# Sister Poppy at the Front

Brenda Gostling and Mik Richardson

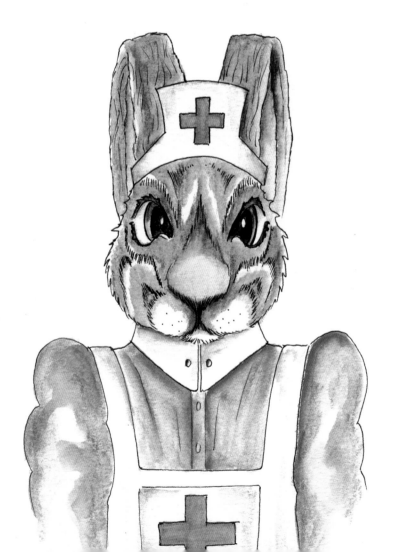

Sister Poppy's story is dedicated to the memory of all the medical teams who served in the First World War, both at home and on the fighting fronts. Our Poppy represents both the trained nurses and the members of the Voluntary Aid Detachment who all faced enormous risk and terrible conditions with bravery and commitment. They were true angels of mercy.

She was inspired in particular by the diaries and letters of nurses like Kate Luard (see kateluard.co.uk) whose wonderful letters home were so revealing about her time on the Western Front.

In addition, here in Norfolk, we have our own nursing heroine, Edith Cavell: her story was the original inspiration for Poppy, Almary Green's GoGoHare sculpture for Break Charity's Norwich trail in 2018 and provided the start of the Sister Poppy journey.

Kindly supported by Break Charity and Almary Green Investments Ltd

Dear Reader

This is a story about Sister Poppy. When we meet her here in this book, she is a nurse caring for wounded soldiers in the First World War in France. She calls the soldiers her "poor boys".

Poppy grew up with her mother and father in a small market town in Norfolk; her father is the local doctor. She's the eldest of three children.

Harry, her brother, is a soldier at the time of this story, serving with the Norfolk Regiment at what was known as the Western Front in France and Belgium.

Poppy's sister, Rose, still lives at home with their parents and Poppy looks forward to her letters.

Poppy trained as a nurse before the war and was one of the first nursing sisters to volunteer to go to help in the hospitals and ambulance stations near the fighting. It's hard work, but Poppy is proud to be doing something to help.

Brenda Gostling 2018

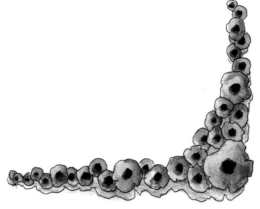

Sister Poppy is very tired. She's been working on her ward all day long, looking after the poor soldiers who've been wounded at the front.

The trenches at the front line are two miles away but Poppy can feel the ground shake here in her bedroom. "Must be dreadful for our poor boys at the battlefield", Poppy thinks.

The guns have been booming for several days now. "Our guns talking to theirs", she tells herself. "No difference really: they speak the same language."

Poppy is billeted in a little cottage, just off the market place in what must have been a pretty French village, before the war. But now the houses around the square are in ruins, damaged by shells some months ago.

Her cottage survived the shelling and Poppy knows she's lucky to have a roof over her head and a proper bed. The poor boys in the trenches are wallowing in mud up to their middles and camping underground in tunnels and dugouts.

Once in her bed, Poppy writes her diary and falls asleep quickly, in spite of the noise of the guns.

She dreams of her home and family back in England. The smell of cut grass drifts into her dream, and the sound of church bells.

She dreams of her mother telling her to wrap up warm and to keep smiling, whatever happens.

She dreams of her brother Harry playing cricket on the lawn and her sister Rose singing as she picks strawberries from the garden.

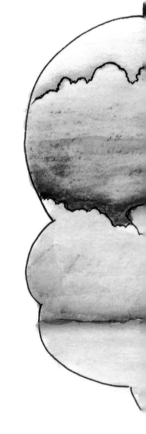

Next morning, Poppy wakes up feeling refreshed and is ready for a new day. Her ward is at a Casualty Clearing Station, a special hospital near the battlefield.

It's the first place that wounded soldiers come to when they're carried away from the front. "There will be lots of new patients today", Poppy thinks, "after all that gunfire last night."

The hospital is in a beautiful French château just outside the village.

When Poppy first arrived, she marvelled at its lovely turrets and balconies but now she doesn't notice them.

Inside, the rooms have been converted into wards, operating theatres and stores for medical supplies.

Poppy has lots to do when new patients arrive. She has to clean their wounds which are often full of mud from the trenches. Then she dresses the wounds with clean bandages.

At the front the soldiers are often dirty and wear the same uniform for days and days as there's no clean water for them to wash or do laundry.

The soldiers who are most badly hurt often need operations and sometimes Poppy helps the doctors in their special operating theatre. It's in what used to be the grand dining room in the château.

Sadly, the soldiers' injuries can be dreadful. Almost every day Poppy sees poor boys having arms or legs amputated because the damage to their bones is so bad.

Poppy knows they can't always save the poor boys with the worst injuries, but they always try.

There are rows and rows of graves marked with wooden crosses in the little graveyard near the church.

On Sundays, Poppy takes flowers there to lay on the graves. Sometimes she sits and cries for all the poor boys who have died so far from home.

It's still early when Poppy gets to her ward. The soldiers who were wounded last night at the front have started to arrive in ambulances and carts, so she's soon busy.

As she bandages one new patient's broken arm, Poppy asks herself "I wonder how many miles of bandages I've used since I came here six months ago? It would probably reach Calais and back."

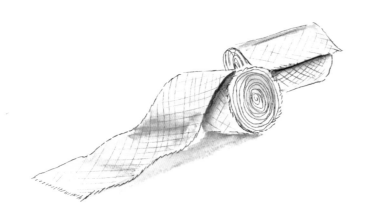

There are often soldiers from far-off places in Poppy's ward too. She's looked after poor boys from India, Australia and Canada who have been fighting with the British Tommies at the front.

Yesterday, many of the wounded soldiers were from Scotland and her ward was full of "och ayes" and "d'ye kens".

Today, the soldiers are from her beloved East Anglia and she feels a little homesick when she hears Norfolk voices around her.

She thinks again of her brother Harry who is fighting somewhere at the front but she doesn't know where.

Sometimes she cares for French people from the village or surrounding farms.

One little boy who came to her ward recently had found an unexploded grenade and took it home to show his mother. Fortunately she managed to throw it into a field before it exploded and the little lad's only injury was a gash on his head made by a stone that flew into the air when it went off.

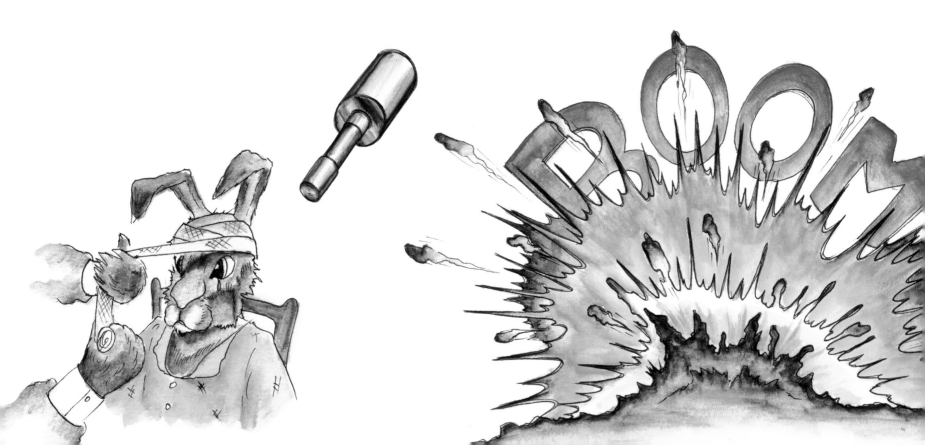

Soldiers come and go from Poppy's ward every day. When they arrive, Poppy cleans their wounds and makes them comfortable. They have a bath and put on clean pyjamas. Poppy can see what a relief it is for her poor boys to be clean again after all the mud in the trenches.

When they leave Poppy's ward, the soldiers go by special ambulance trains from the station in the town nearby.

The trains also bring stocks of medicines and bandages.

On a good day the trains bring the mail as well, with letters and parcels from home.

Today is a good day and Poppy has a letter from her mother.
She tucks it into her apron pocket to read later.

Her mother has also sent a box of things for Poppy to give to her patients. Poppy can't wait to see her poor boys' faces light up when she gives them the socks and mufflers to keep them warm.

Poppy smiles to herself as she thinks of her mother and her sister sitting around the fire at home, busily knitting for the brave boys at the front.

Her mother has also sent some writing sets for the soldiers. Poppy knows these will be received with big smiles. Letters are really important to the soldiers who are so far away from home.

When she has time, Poppy writes letters for the poor boys who are too ill to do it themselves to send home to their mothers, wives and sweethearts.

Today, there is no time to do anything except look after the soldiers' wounds. Soon every bed in her ward is full and there are more soldiers on stretchers between the beds.

Poppy chats to several of the soldiers who tell her that the battle is going well at the front but that both sides have seen lots of their men killed or wounded.

Poppy wonders when it will all end. "Such a waste of these poor boys' lives", she thinks. "And there will be wards like mine on the other side of the front line too with poor German boys suffering as much as our brave boys".

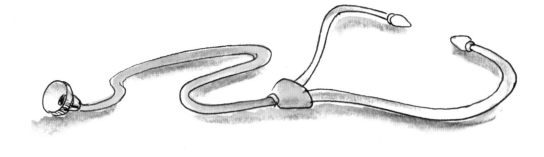

Poppy is busy giving medicine to one of the soldiers when she hears someone shout "Poppy!" from across the ward.

She's surprised at hearing her name as the soldiers usually only call her "Sister" or "Nurse". She looks up and sees that a young soldier has been brought into the ward on a stretcher.

His face is covered in mud, but she recognises him straightaway. It's her brother Harry!

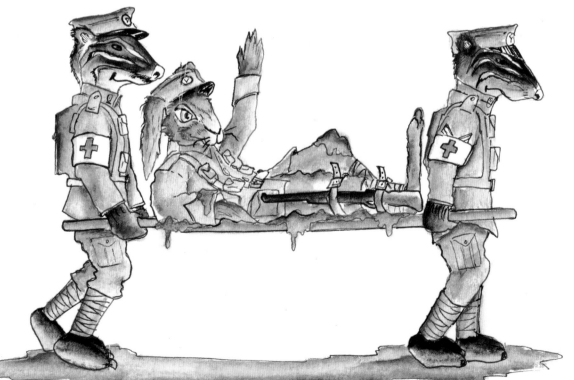

Poppy's first happiness at seeing Harry is replaced with worry. Is he badly wounded? She is soon reassured: Harry has a broken leg, but it doesn't look too serious.

Harry tells Poppy that he was at the top of the steps of his dugout when a shell landed nearby and the walls of the trench collapsed, sending him falling down the steps.

He broke his leg as he fell and then was buried in mud. Luckily other soldiers saw what happened and rushed to dig him out.

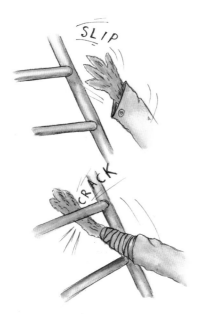

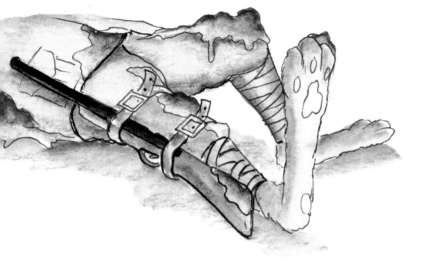

A Medical Officer was nearby and as soon as Harry was pulled out, he made a splint for Harry's leg using his rifle and two soldiers' belts.

Poppy is relieved that Harry received treatment so quickly. Getting a splint onto his leg straightaway will make it more likely that the bone will heal properly.

All that Harry needs now is to have the splint replaced and properly bandaged. Poppy helps clean him up and gives him a big hug.

Harry is more concerned about getting a nice cup of tea and a piece of cake. "We haven't had cake in our trench for three weeks", he tells Poppy.

Poppy has to go back to looking after the other poor boys for the rest of the afternoon. Every time she passes Harry, she gives him a smile and a wave, but there's no time to talk properly.

Finally, the stretchers stop arriving and the wards settle down for the night. For Poppy, it's the end of her shift and she would normally go back to her billet to have her tea and sleep.

Tonight she has other plans. As soon as she hands care of the ward over to the Night Sister, she hurries back to Harry's bed.

"It's funny", she thinks. "I've stopped being a nursing sister for the night and now I'm being Harry's sister".

Harry is delighted when Poppy pulls their mother's letter out of her apron pocket.

Together they read the news from home and talk about family days gone by.

Poppy is happy because she knows that Harry will be sent home so that his leg can heal properly. He'll go on tomorrow's train to the main hospital, then he will probably be sent on a hospital ship back to England.

She hopes that by the time Harry's leg is better, the war will be over.

Harry is happy to be going home, but can't stop worrying about the other soldiers in his regiment who are still at the front.

"I have to come back as soon as I can", he tells Poppy.
"They need every man they can get".

Poppy grabs one of the new writing cases and writes a quick letter to her mother for Harry to take home.

Later, as she walks back to her billet, Poppy suddenly realises that the guns are quiet tonight.

She knows that it doesn't mean that the war has ended yet, but at least it will mean there will be fewer poor boys coming to her ward tomorrow.

In her bed, even without the noise of the guns, Poppy is finding it hard to sleep.

"What a day it has been!", she thinks. "And how many more days will there be before we can all go home again?"

At last she falls asleep and dreams again of cricket and strawberries and all the sights and sounds of home.

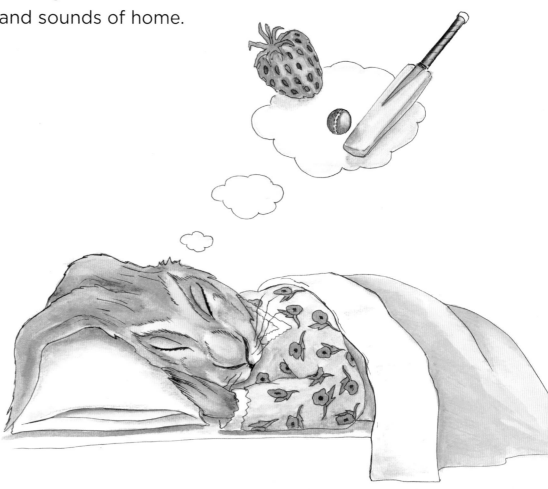

# GoGoHares 2018, Break Charity and Almary Green

Sister Poppy's story was inspired by Poppy the GoGoHare sponsored by Norwich-based Independent Financial Advisers, Almary Green, for Norfolk's GoGoHares 2018 Sculpture Trail raising funds for children, young people and families charity, Break.

The concept of Poppy GoGoHare as a First World War nurse came out of discussions between Mik Richardson, the artist commissioned to paint Almary Green's hare; Brenda Gostling, Almary Green's Marketing Consultant and now Sister Poppy author, and Almary Green's Managing Director, Carl Lamb who wanted the firm's GoGoHare to commemorate the centenary of the end of WW1.

The GoGoHares 2018 Sculpture Trail is to be held in Summer 2018 and is presented by Break Charity in partnership with Wild in Art. It comprises 50 hare sculptures around the city of Norwich plus 18 hares around the county of Norfolk. Brenda and Mik will donate a share of the net profits of this book to Break Charity.

Break celebrates its 50th anniversary in 2018 with the ethos of the charity remaining unchanged: to support vulnerable children, young people and families. It provides small scale children's homes, a fostering service and support for young care leavers. In addition, it delivers respite breaks for children with disabilities and support for children and families through the Break Family Centre. See www.break-charity.org.